BRETT FAVRE

The All-Time Leader

To Steele, the only person I know who loves sports more than I do, and to our friends at Josie Woods, for putting on every game for us to watch.—L.M.

GROSSET & DUNLAP
Published by the Penguin Group
Penguin Group (USA) Inc., 375 Hudson Street, New York, New York 10014, USA
Penguin Group (Canada), 90 Eglinton Avenue East, Suite 700, Toronto,
Ontario M4P 2Y3, Canada
(a division of Pearson Penguin Canada Inc.)
Penguin Books Ltd., 80 Strand, London WC2R 0RL, England
Penguin Group Ireland, 25 St. Stephen's Green, Dublin 2, Ireland
(a division of Penguin Books Ltd.)
Penguin Group (Australia), 250 Camberwell Road, Camberwell, Victoria 3124, Australia
(a division of Pearson Australia Group Pty. Ltd.)
Penguin Books India Pvt. Ltd., 11 Community Centre, Panchsheel Park,
New Delhi—110 017, India
Penguin Group (NZ), 67 Apollo Drive, Rosedale, North Shore 0632, New Zealand
(a division of Pearson New Zealand Ltd.)
Penguin Books (South Africa) (Pty.) Ltd., 24 Sturdee Avenue,
Rosebank, Johannesburg 2196, South Africa

Penguin Books Ltd., Registered Offices:
80 Strand, London WC2R 0RL, England

Photo credits: cover: © Morry Gash/AP Images; copyright page: © Jonathan Daniel/Getty Images; title page: © Morry Gash/AP Images; page 5: © Morry Gash/AP Images; page 6: © Mike Roemer/ AP Images; page 7: © Jed Jacobsohn/Getty Images; page 9: © Morry Gash/AP Images; page 15: © Ronald C. Modra/*Sports Illustrated*; page 17: © AP Photo/University of Southern Mississippi, Steve Rouse; page 18: © All Sport/All Sport; pages 19-23: © Allen Steele/Getty Images; pages 25-27: © Morry Gash/AP Images; page 30: © Messerschmidt/NFL/Getty Images; page 31: © Mike Roemer/AP Images; page 32: © Jonathan Daniel/Getty Images; page 34: © Jim Mone/AP Images; page 36: © AP Photo/University of Southern Mississippi, Steve Rouse; page 37: © Morry Gash/AP Images; page 38: © Mary Butkis/AP Images; page 41: © George Napolitano/Film Magic; page 42: © Mike Roemer/AP Images; page 43: © Morry Gash/AP Images; page 44: © AP Photo/*Racine Journal Times*, Mark Hertzberg; page 47: © Morry Gash/AP Images.

Library of Congress Control Number: 2008006657

ISBN 978-0-448-44978-4   10 9 8 7 6 5 4 3 2 1

BRETT FAVRE
The All-Time Leader

By Laura Marchesani
with photographs

Grosset & Dunlap

On Top of the World

It was September 30, 2007. The Green Bay Packers were playing the Minnesota Vikings on a Sunday afternoon.

The first quarter began with a giant cheer from the crowd. Even though the Vikings were the home team, the stadium was filled with Green Bay's colors: mustard yellow and green. Thousands of Packers fans, known as Cheeseheads, had traveled all the way from Green Bay for the opportunity to watch their quarterback, Brett Favre, make football history.

The first quarter was ticking by. There was no score. With less than seven minutes left in the quarter, the Packers offense took the field. Quarterback Brett Favre took his position. His mind was completely focused. After sixteen years of playing in the NFL,

Fans cheer for their favorite team.

Brett knew how to drown out the noise of over 60,000 screaming fans.

There were only sixteen more yards until the goal line. *Snap!* Brett held the ball for just a few seconds before passing it to his teammate. But the Packers didn't gain any extra yards on the play. If the Packers didn't score a touchdown here, they'd be forced to settle for a field goal.

Brett huddled with his teammates, going over the next play. The huddle broke with a *clap*!

Just before his teammate hiked him the ball, Brett noticed that the Vikings defense was lining up for a blitz. A blitz is when the defense puts more coverage on the quarterback instead of covering other players on the team, hoping to tackle the quarterback before he can throw the ball. Quickly, Brett called a different play to beat

Favre gathers his team in for a huddle.

the blitz. There was no time for another huddle. So Brett ran up and down the offensive line, telling his teammates the new play. Brett's plan was risky, but it had to be done. If his teammates didn't understand the play, or couldn't hear what Brett was saying, the play could fall apart.

Tick. The play clock was winding down, and Brett was almost out of time. Just as the play clock was about to hit zero, Brett threw the ball to a teammate on the five-yard line, who ran straight into the end zone.

Brett didn't see the catch, but he could tell from the cheering fans that it was a touchdown. Every single person in the stadium began cheering Brett's name. Brett Favre had just broken the all-time NFL career passing touchdown record by

Favre's teammates lift him into the air to celebrate his touchdown pass.

throwing his 421st touchdown to teammate Greg Jennings!

Brett ran down the field with his index finger pointed to the sky. The whole stadium celebrated as Brett's teammates lifted him into the air.

At age 37, everyone said that Brett was too old to play football, but he definitely proved them wrong.

Brett's Beginnings

Brett Lorenzo Favre's story begins on October 10, 1969, in Gulfport, Mississippi. Brett weighed 9 pounds 15 ounces when he was born. When Brett was still a baby, his parents, Bonita and Big Irv, along with his older brother Scott, moved to the small town of Kiln, Mississippi. It was there that Brett's younger brother Jeff and his younger sister Brandi were born.

Growing up, Brett lived on a 52-and-a-half acre property, so Brett and his siblings didn't have any neighbors close by to play with. Instead, the Favre boys made up games to pass the time. They got into trouble for making a game of throwing rocks at each other.

Brett's dad coached high school

football and American Legion baseball
in Kiln. And as soon as Brett was old
enough, he tagged along with Big Irv to
sporting events. All three of the Favre
boys played Pee Wee football and Little
League baseball. In football, Brett and
his brothers were always bigger and
better than all the other kids. In Little
League, some of the players on opposing
teams refused to bat against Brett because

they were afraid of getting hit by Brett's blazing fastball!

At Hancock North Central High School, Brett played football, but baseball was actually his better sport. Brett started for the varsity baseball team when he was only an eighth grader. During one of Brett's best baseball games, he hit a double in his first time at the plate and a home run in his second at-bat. When Brett came to the plate for the third time, he let three balls go by, and reached out to hit the fourth ball. He sent the ball over the right-field fence!

All three Favre boys were quarterbacks on the high school football team. Brett was the middle child and wanted to follow in his older brother's footsteps by being a quarterback. Brett was big enough to be a linebacker, but his dad put him at quarterback because he knew Brett would come to every practice and game. Brett wasn't known as the best quarterback ever to play on Big Irv's team. According to some football fans, Brett's older brother, Scott, was thought to be a better quarterback than Brett!

Near the end of Brett's last season at Hancock North Central, Big Irv asked a football scout from the University of Southern Mississippi to come watch Brett play. The scout watched Brett help his team win the game. But afterward, he told Big Irv that he couldn't recommend Brett for a spot on the Southern Mississippi team. He said he hadn't seen him throw the ball enough. Big Irv asked the scout to come back again the following week, and he did. Eventually, Southern Mississippi offered Brett a scholarship to play on

their team as a defenseman. Brett gladly
accepted. It was his only scholarship offer
from a college! His family was excited for
him to take this next step in his career.

Even though Brett loved playing
baseball, he wanted to follow in his
brother's footsteps and play college
football. Scott had gone on to play
quarterback for Mississippi State after
high school. Brett left for Southern

Mississippi with high expectations, but he had no idea what was in store for him when he got there.

On the Sidelines

Brett was on his way to Hattiesburg, Mississippi, to play for the University of Southern Mississippi Golden Eagles. The coach wanted Brett to play defensive back, but Brett was determined to be the quarterback. The coach finally granted Brett's wish and allowed him to be the quarterback—on the seventh string!

In the first game of the season, the Golden Eagles lost a game to their rivals,

The University of Southern Mississippi marching band performs at halftime.

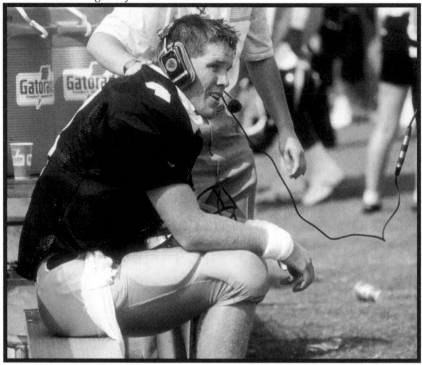

Favre watches the game from the sidelines.

Alabama, 38–6. Two weeks later, Southern Mississippi played Tulane at their home field, known as "The Rock." Brett was still frustrated about being stuck on the seventh string. He was used to being the star of the team, and for the first time in his life, he was sitting on the sidelines.

The Golden Eagles struggled early in the game. The coach was so frustrated with his team's performance that he did something that shocked all of Brett's teammates *and* the fans watching the game: He put Brett into the game as quarterback! He wanted to see how well Brett could respond to the pressure. Brett knew that this was his shot to prove to everyone that he deserved to be on the team.

When Brett walked out onto the field, the fans cheered loudly. The university was just over fifty miles away from Kiln, so many of the people in the stands had watched Brett play in high school and knew how well he could play.

The Golden Eagles were down 24–17, but once Brett took the field, the entire pace of the game changed. Brett was only 17 years old, but in the offensive huddle he told the other players, "I'm in charge now." Brett started throwing passes to his teammates, and the team charged toward the end zone. Brett threw two touchdown passes to lead his team to a 31–24 victory!

That victory won Brett a starting quarterback spot for the next four years. Going into his senior season, Brett was on top of the world—and his game. His fans and his teammates loved him, and

he was on course to break multiple school records. Brett was so popular that a sports director at the school had organized a "Favre 4 Heisman" campaign, hoping to gain support for Brett's run for the Heisman Trophy next year. The Heisman is the award given to the best college football player of the year. But all of that changed when Brett was involved in a near-fatal car accident during the summer before his senior year.

After a day on Ship Island, a vacation spot off the coast of Mississippi, Brett almost collided with an oncoming car and flipped. The first question he asked his mother in the ambulance was, "Will I be able to play football again?" Brett knew there were only a few weeks before the start of training camp, and he wanted to get back out onto the field.

Brett suffered serious injuries and had to have surgery on his stomach. But he refused to give up. Four weeks later, Brett was back in the lineup and led the Golden Eagles to a 27–24 win over Alabama.

Brett started every game for the rest of the season despite the accident and the operation. Having him on the field gave the team strength, because Brett was their leader. Brett graduated after four years with several school records to his name, including the record for career touchdown passes and career passing yards. Southern Mississippi wasn't known as a major football powerhouse, but while Brett was there, the team beat their rivals Auburn and Alabama and went to two bowl games. Brett worked his way up from backup quarterback to the school hero. Now he was ready to take on the NFL.

Rise to Greatness

In the second round of the 1991 NFL Draft, the Atlanta Falcons drafted Brett, the thirty-third overall pick. The first pass that Brett ever threw in a regular season NFL game resulted in the other team scoring a touchdown. Brett only threw four passes in his career at Atlanta, and none of them were completions. Brett started to feel the way he did during

his first weeks at Southern Mississippi—frustrated, but determined to prove that he was the best.

Brett was traded to the Green Bay Packers after the 1991 season. The Packers' manager had seen Brett play and singled him out as the next great NFL quarterback. Brett was happy to leave the Falcons and get a second chance to show the world what he could do. The Packers' coach saw potential in Brett, and gave him the backup quarterback job once he arrived in Green Bay.

It was the second game of the 1992 season, and the Packers were playing the Tampa Bay Buccaneers. At halftime, the Buccaneers were up 17–0. The Packers' head coach decided to bench the starting quarterback, Don Majkowski, and put Brett in the game to see what he

could do. In his first play of the game, Brett fired a pass. The football hit a defenseman and bounced back to Brett. He caught the ball and was immediately tackled for a loss of seven yards! The fans booed Brett's mistake, and the Packers eventually lost the game 31–3.

In the third game of the season, the Packers' starting quarterback suffered an ankle injury that would put him on the sidelines for four weeks. The coach put Brett back in the game. During the course of the game, Brett made mistake after mistake. He looked so bad on the field that the Packers fans chanted, "Take him out! Take him out!" But Brett wasn't ready to give up just yet. He knew that he was good enough to bring home a victory.

With a minute left in the game, the Packers were down 23–17. The Packers offense was lined up on their own eight-yard line—they had to go ninety-two yards for a touchdown! Brett took a deep breath, and threw the football as hard as he could, hoping that his aim was on. The crowd erupted in cheers— Brett had completed a forty-two-yard pass! On the next play, Brett threw the game-winning touchdown pass with only thirteen seconds left in the game.

Since then, Brett has been a hero to the people of Green Bay. He continued to make amazing plays and win games. After that game, on September 20, 1992, Brett started every game at quarterback in Green Bay, setting an NFL record for most consecutive starts. And after his very first season, Brett was voted to the Pro Bowl alongside other legendary quarterbacks, like Steve Young and Troy Aikman. Brett was also the youngest player to ever be voted to the Pro Bowl, the NFL's all-star game.

Before Brett came to Green Bay, the Packers were not a great team. Since Brett took over the starting quarterback job, the Packers have had much better success on the field. They have gone to two Super Bowls, with a victory in 1997

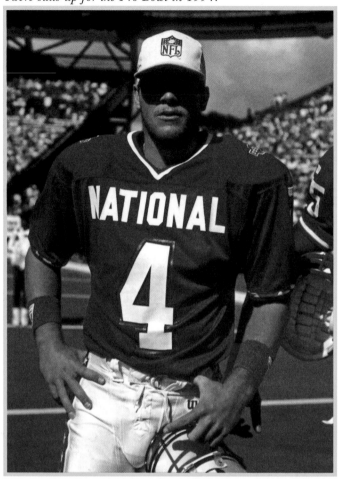

Favre suits up for the Pro Bowl in 1994.

over the New England Patriots. Brett was voted the NFL MVP three times. He is the face of football in Green Bay, a city that loves its team so much that the waiting list for season tickets is over 57,000 names long—a thirty-year wait!

Up Close and Personal

Throughout his life, Brett has been a family man. In 1996, Brett married Deanna Tynes, his high school sweetheart. The two met when Brett was only 7 years old. Brett and Deanna have two daughters together, Brittany and Breleigh. While building his own family, Brett continued to have a close relationship

Brett celebrates with his wife Deanna after a playoff game on January 12, 2008.

with his parents, Big Irv and Bonita. That's why Brett was heartbroken when his dad, Big Irv, passed away on December 21, 2003.

The day after Brett's father died, the Packers were scheduled to play a *Monday Night Football* game against the Oakland Raiders. Brett had a decision to make: play the game, or take the night off to

Brett walks off the field with his wife Deanna and daughters, Brittany and Breleigh.

be with his family. Brett must have been overwhelmed by grief, but he was determined not to let his *football* family down. Big Irv had given Brett his competitive spirit, and taught him never to give up, even when times are tough. Brett knew what he had to do: He would play in the game, and dedicate it to his dad.

Brett was nervous going into the game. Throughout his childhood, every time Brett stepped onto the field, he wanted to please Big Irv. And now, Brett wanted it more than ever. The game was aired internationally, and fans everywhere watched to see how Brett would rise to the challenge. The December 22, 2003 game against the Oakland Raiders was the defining moment of Brett's career and one of the best games he has ever played. Brett passed for four touchdowns in the first half, and finished the game with 399 total yards in a 41–7 win over the Raiders.

Brett was named the NFC Offensive Player of the Week for his performance in that game. Even the Raiders fans,

who are tough on visiting teams, were rooting for Brett. Later that year, Brett was awarded a coveted ESPY Award for his *Monday Night Football* performance.

The months after Big Irv's death were tough. Brett and his family faced several tragedies. But Brett refused to let those hard times bring him down. He focused on three major things: football, his family, and working with charities.

When Brett was younger, he befriended a mentally disabled man who was the equipment manager for his Little League team. When he was older, Brett decided to start a charity to help disabled kids in Mississippi and Wisconsin: the Brett Favre Fourward Foundation.

After Hurricane Katrina, Brett used the Packers' postgame press conferences to rally support for the victims. He also

Deanna speaks at her Walk for Life fund-raiser.

donated his time once a week when he was playing at home to the Make-A-Wish Foundation, and helped Deanna found a charity to raise money for the victims of breast cancer. He did all this while continuing to play his hardest in every Packers game. However, the 2005 season was a disappointing one for Packers fans, and ended without the Packers making the playoffs. Many people thought that Brett would retire. After all, he was 36 years old, well past the usual retirement age in the NFL. He had already won a Super Bowl and three MVP awards. If Brett retired, he would go down as the best quarterback in Packers history.

Favre celebrates his 420th touchdown pass. He tied Dan Marino's NFL record in this 2007 game against the San Diego Chargers!

The End of an Era

The fans in the Packers' stadium, Lambeau Field, were screaming as loud as they could. Some waved homemade banners and others showed their team spirit with painted faces. It was the home opener for the Packers' 2007 season, and the energy inside the stadium was electric.

The Packers were back in action with Brett Favre leading the way. During the

off-season, everyone wondered whether or not Brett would retire. Brett was 37 years old—only ten years younger than the NFL's current oldest player.

After the first possession, the Packers punted the ball to the Philadelphia Eagles. The Eagles player caught the ball and started to run. But the Packers defense tackled the runner, and he dropped the ball. The Packers picked the ball up and took off toward the end zone: touchdown! The roar from the Cheeseheads in the stands was deafening. Brett Favre cheered along from the sidelines. Everyone wondered if this was where Brett was meant to be: on the sidelines, instead of in the game?

Instead of thinking about all the people who thought he was too old to be out there, Brett concentrated on playing the best football he could in the 2007 season. His focus paid off. Along with breaking the record for most career passing touchdowns, Brett also broke the record for most career wins, with 149 on September 16, 2007. In November 2007, Brett became only the third NFL quarterback to have defeated all thirty-one other NFL teams. Brett also won the *Sports Illustrated* Sportsman of the Year award for 2007, a high honor that has only been given to four previous NFL players.

While Brett had an amazing individual season, the Packers had an even better season as a team. The Packers finished the regular season with a 13-3 record and easily came out on top of the NFC North, with big wins over rivals Minnesota and Detroit. The Packers had finished the 2006 season with an 8-8

record. No one expected them to be the team to beat in the 2007 season. But the Packers continued to win games, and finished the regular season with the second-best record in the NFC. This gave them an automatic place in the second round of the playoffs.

In their first playoff game, the Packers played the Seattle Seahawks. Despite the snow that pounded down on the players during the game, the Packers won 42–20. Brett completed eighteen out of twenty-three passes for a total of 173 yards, and threw three touchdowns. Brett's age and experience helped him

break another record: He became only
the second passer in the history of the
NFL with over 5,000 yards in postseason
play!

The next week, the Packers played
in the NFC Championship game against
the New York Giants. The Packers were
only one win away from the Super Bowl!
During the game, the temperature in
Lambeau Field was as cold as -3 degrees
Fahrenheit. It was the third-coldest game

in NFL history! Brett and his teammates knew this would be a tough one to win.

After four quarters of football, the score was tied 20–20. The game went into overtime. The first team to score would win the game. The Packers had the ball, but Brett threw an interception, and the Giants gained possession. The Giants tried to get as close to the end zone as they could, but were unsuccessful twice. Then the Giants quarterback threw an incomplete pass. So the Giants tried to

Fans brave the cold to watch the Packers earn a trip to the Super Bowl.

win the game with a field goal . . . and they did. New York won the game 23–20. Brett and the Packers weren't going to the Super Bowl. Even though his team lost the game, Brett still managed to set another record. Brett threw a touchdown pass in the game, making it his eighteenth postseason game with a touchdown.

After the game, everyone wondered if this was finally the right time for Brett to retire. Quarterback Dan Marino retired when he was 38, the same age as Brett. Plus, Brett had already broken most of the major records for quarterbacks in the NFL, and was a shoo-in for the Hall of Fame. The people of Green Bay loved Brett. They even named the street in front of the Packers' stadium Brett Favre Pass! If Brett retired now, he would go out on top of the world.

And on March 4, 2008, Brett finally decided to retire after seventeen years in the NFL. Favre announced that he would finally "hang up his cleats." In an NFL press conference, Brett emotionally thanked his teammates and his fans for such a great career. He said he had given everything he could to his team over the past seventeen years. After an incredible season in which Favre continued to set more league records, his teammates were shocked . . . people wondered if Brett would stick to his decision as the next season approached.

Fans had a hard time believing that this was Favre's last year, but they knew one thing for sure: Brett Favre will go down in the record books as one of the most unforgettable quarterbacks in NFL history. But more importantly, he will be remembered as a leader who played with passion. Brett's teammates and coaches looked up to him for advice and inspiration on the field, and that is the most important achievement of all.

Brett Favre's Record Book

★ Only quarterback in the NFL to be a three-time MVP

★ Was selected to play in the Pro Bowl nine times in his career

★ Most consecutive starts of any quarterback in the NFL (253)

★ Most career completions (5,377)

Brett Favre's 2007 Records

★ Most career touchdown passes (442)

★ Most career wins as a starting quarterback (160)

★ Most career pass attempts (8,758)

★ Most career passing yards (61,655)

★ One of three players in the NFL to have defeated all thirty-one other teams

★ Named Sportsman of the Year by *Sports Illustrated*

★ Became the second passer in the history of the NFL with over 5,000 yards in postseason play

★ Played eighteen straight postseason games with at least one completed touchdown pass